10 Minute Histories

STONE CIRCLES

D1343980

First published in 2006 by English Heritage

ISBN-10: 1 85074 928 0
ISBN-13: 978 1 85074 928 8
Product code: 50971

Copyright text © Caroline Crewe-Read, 2006
Copyright illustrations © Fiona Powers, 2006

10 9 8 7 6 5 4 3 2 1

All rights reserved. No part of this publication may be reproduced,
stored in a retrieval system or transmitted in any form or by any means,
electronic, mechanical, photocopying, recording or otherwise without
the prior permission of the publisher.

Written by: Caroline Crewe-Read
Designer: Fiona Powers
Editor: Beck Ward Murphy

Printed in Croatia by Zrinski

*Dedicated to Ronald Hutton and Chris Chippindale, for their inspirational
teaching, to my parents, Ann and Leslie McKinnes, for the opportunities they
have given me and for the endless games of hide-and-seek played at
Castlerigg, and to my husband Nigel, for his answering support and
encouragement in all that* ...

MORAY COUNCIL
LIBRARIES &
INFO.SERVICES

20 19 08 58	
Askews	
J930.1	

10 Minute Histories

STONE CIRCLES

ENGLISH HERITAGE

Contents

Introduction

magine hauling a 40-ton stone up a hill with no big trucks, no cranes and no computer technology to help you. Sounds tough, doesn't it? Where would you start? It seems almost impossible...but that's exactly what hard-working communities of people did thousands of years ago to build one of the most amazing stone monuments ever – Stonehenge!

Stone circles

Stonehenge is a stone circle. It's just one of nearly 1,000 ancient stone circles that are scattered all over the UK. Who built these incredible structures and why are they different shapes? What were they used for and what do they mean to us today?

Ancient builders

Well, it all started over 5,000 years ago in prehistory when our ancestors – the Neolithic people – lived in Britain. They built the first stone circles, many of which are still standing today. They were artistic, creative people and highly skilled workmen who designed and built all sorts of different monuments.

Ideas from abroad?

For a long time, historians and **archaeologists** thought that our ancestors weren't clever enough to build such huge and difficult things. How could they move the enormous stones so far, for example, and how did they make the stones stand up on their ends? Instead, it was thought that stone circles must have been built by knowledgeable foreigners who introduced their imaginative ideas to this country.

Giant ideas

Some people even thought that stone circles were built by giants, or that they were people who had been turned to stone for doing bad things. These beliefs led to many strange rumours and legends about the origins and uses of stone circles.

Sky gazing

There may have been lots of different reasons why stone circles were built. Some archaeologists think that they were built so that prehistoric people could use them to watch the movements of the sun, moon and stars. This movement would have told them what time of year it was. Neolithic and Bronze Age people were farmers and so would have been very interested in the changing of the seasons.

Knowing when the longest and shortest days of the year were would have helped people plan when to plough their fields or plant crops. You can find out more about why stone circles were built as you read on...

> **NOTE**
> Words in bold can be found in the glossary on page 81.

All shapes and sizes

Not all stone circles are circles, believe it or not. Some are shaped like ovals and others, like Arbor Low, right, are even egg-shaped. The size and type of circles built may have depended on the size of the community that built them, what they were to be used for and how many people needed to fit inside.

Archaeology

The people who built stone circles couldn't write, so what we know now about stone sites comes from the evidence that **archaeology** gives us. Archaeologists use lots of different methods to help them look at and collect information about monuments like stone circles. They often have to rely on physical evidence, like this skeleton found at Avebury, below, to help them make sense of the stone circles themselves.

Archaeology can't tell us everything, though, and so your thoughts and guesses about a stone circle's purpose could be just as good as that of an expert!

Famous chaps from the past

John Aubrey, left, and William Stukeley, right, were two famous historians. A huge amount of what we know today about stone circles has come from their hard work and investigations in the 17th and 18th centuries.

Dates in prehistory

At one time in Britain there would have been over 3,000 stone circles. They were built during prehistoric times, over a period of 2,000 years, during either the Neolithic or Bronze Age.

Prehistory is the period in the past before writing had been invented. In Britain, the prehistoric period ended when the Romans invaded in AD 43. They brought with them the power of writing so that a written record – called history – could be kept. This means that we know far more about what has happened since the Roman invasion than before it in prehistory.

We divide prehistory into three main sections: the Stone Age, the Bronze Age and the Iron Age. The Stone Age on its own covers a very long period of time so it is divided up further into three periods – the Palaeolithic, the Mesolithic and the Neolithic. Each of these periods uses the same ending in their names – 'lithic' – from the Greek word lithos, meaning stone. The rough dates for these different ages are:

- ◎ **Stone Age: Palaeolithic .... before 10,000 BC**

- ◎ **Stone Age: Mesolithic .... 10,000 BC–4400 BC**

- ◎ **Stone Age: Neolithic .... 4400 BC–2500 BC**
  You can read more about Neolithic life on page 15.

- ◎ **Bronze Age .... 2500 BC–800 BC**
  This was a time when people started to use bronze for tools and weapons, like these shown right. You can read more about Bronze Age life on page 37.

- ◎ **Iron Age .... 800 BC–AD 43**
  This is the final period of prehistory. Iron took over from bronze as the preferred metal for all sorts of different tools, weapons and everyday objects.

Stone circle sites

Key

1 Castlerigg

2 Long Meg

3 Swinside

4 Arbor Low

5 Tregeseal East

6 Rollright Stones

7 Stanton Drew

8 Grey Croft

9 Little Meg

10 Glassonby

11 Druid's Temple

12 Boscawen-un

13 Merry Maidens

14 The Hurlers

15 Duloe

16 Nine Stones, Altarnun

17 Grey Wethers

18 Merrivale

19 Mitchell's Fold

20 Nine Stone Close

21 Nine Ladies

22 Doll Tor

23 Three Kings

24 Avebury

25 Stonehenge

INVERNESS

STIRLING

GLASGOW

EDINBURGH

18

13 2

12

8 1

3

11

YORK

LEEDS

MANCHESTER

21

4 22

20

19

NORWICH

BIRMINGHAM

6

CARDIFF

OXFORD

BRISTOL

7 24

LONDON

25

SOUTHAMPTON

16

14 17

23

5 15

9 10 PLYMOUTH

Building a stone circle

Building a stone circle would have taken a lot of careful planning. The site, size and shape would be agreed first. Sometimes, at this point, builders would also know which special features they might want, such as **outlying stones**. Next, the really hard work would start: deep holes would be dug in the ground using stone axes or antler picks, like the ones shown right. It was important that the holes were deep enough to stop the stones from falling over.

Moving stones

The stones used for almost all of the circles in Britain would have been found fairly close to the site chosen for the circle. Even so, moving the stones these short distances would have been no mean feat. Some archaeologists think that stones would have been placed on a wooden sledge and dragged, either by men or cattle, along a track of timber rollers, as shown, left. As the sledge moved over the rollers, a group of men carried the rollers from the back to the front and so the journey continued. It must have taken quite some time to cover even a short distance, though.

Finishing touches

Once they had arrived on site, some stones would have been light enough for only a few people to heave into position. Others would have needed a much greater effort. Ropes were probably used to make a pulley system and stones would have been hauled up and levered into position by a larger group of workers. Once upright in the **foundation** holes, materials such as earth, clay and small stones would have been used to wedge the standing stones firmly in place.

Castlerigg

Age: Neolithic
Location: Cumbria
Size of circle: 33m x 30m
Tallest stone 2.5m
Heaviest stone: 16 tons
Made from: slate
No. of stones: 38 remain today (originally 52)

Huddled among the dramatic fells and mountains of the Lake District is an amazing stone circle called Castlerigg. It's one of the most well-known and best-preserved circles in Cumbria and thought to be one of the earliest circles ever built in Britain. It's extremely important in stone circle circles!

The amazing views from magical Castlerigg across to the mountains.

Mysterious shapes

Castlerigg isn't actually circular in shape at all. It's more like a wonky circle with one flat side. Perhaps prehistoric builders made one side flat on purpose, or perhaps they had not had enough practice in laying out proper circles by this time.

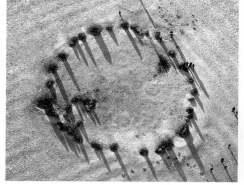

An aerial photograph of Castlerigg in the snow.

The rectangle

A mysterious rectangle of stones sits inside the main circle – a feature that you cannot find at any other stone circle in Britain. Despite doing many excavations, archaeologists still haven't found anything interesting buried inside this rectangle other than a deep pit filled with charcoal, which was discovered in 1882.

Was this rectangle of stones originally a tomb?

People would have entered the stone circle between these two tall stones.

The way in

The entrance to Castlerigg is on the north side of the circle. It's made from two stones that are much taller than the others.

Guess what?

In 1919 a man reported seeing a spooky light in the sky over Castlerigg stone circle. He didn't think it was a UFO though! Instead, he believed that the light was a natural event that was common to the area. This could be true. Castlerigg sits on rocks that have a geological fault in them. Scientists believe that when these rocks are under huge pressure they can make electrical discharges that look like lightning. Perhaps the builders of Castlerigg thought that the location of this site was important because of this? We still don't know…it's a mystery!

Place of peace?

Archaeologists believe that Neolithic people deliberately built this particular circle in such a beautiful place because one of its uses may have been as a **sanctuary**.

◎ Castlerigg may have been used in different ways at different times.

Prehistoric shopping

Three stone axes have been found at Castlerigg, so it's likely that this site was used as a market place for trading tools – even Neolithic people liked to shop! In prehistoric times, there were many stone-axe works nearby, so this circle may have been an important meeting place for traders. Axes have also been found at another Cumbrian circle, Long Meg and her Daughters (*see* pages 16–19) – perhaps traders met here before travelling south with their wares.

◎ These axe heads found at Stonehenge are similar to the ones found at Castlerigg.

It's magic!

Another stone circle near to Castlerigg – Elva Plain – also has connections with axes, as polished prehistoric stone axes were also discovered there. Over the years axes were commonly thought to have magical properties. Even as recently as the 19th century, farmers in western Europe believed that stone axes were thunderbolts sent from the heavens!

◎ The stone circle builders would probably have looked just like us. They were probably a lot fitter, though, because of their active, outdoor life.

Neolithic life

The Neolithic period began around 4400 BC, nearly one thousand years before the first stone circle was built. During this time people started to use stone to make objects and tools for use in and around the home, although wood was still a very important material.

Neolithic people didn't live for very long. Most men would only have lived until they were 30 or 35 years old, and women might have reached the age of 25 or 30 years old. Life was hard for these people, especially for children, and large numbers of them died during this period.

We don't really know much about the type of homes that Neolithic people lived in. Evidence from archaeology tells us that their huts were probably shaped like rectangles, but we still don't know what these houses were like inside or anything about their furniture.

Neolithic people began to rely less on hunting as a way of finding food and started to clear woods so that they could keep animals such as cows, pigs, sheep and goats. They also began to grow crops, such as wheat and barley, which were used for making bread.

The introduction of this kind of farming during the Neolithic meant that people were settling in the same place for longer periods of time. Although each individual settlement, or village, would have been quite small, there would have been contact between communities. People may have met up to trade goods or to celebrate seasonal festivals. It may be that Neolithic people wanted to start building permanent structures such as stone circles because they were putting down roots and staking a claim to a particular area.

Long Meg and her Daughters

Age: Neolithic
Location: Cumbria
Size of circle: 109.4m x 93m
Tallest stone: 3.7m
Heaviest stone: 29 tons
Made from: red sandstone and local granite
No. of stones: 71

How many children are in your family? Two? Three? Four, perhaps? Imagine having a family with over 70 children in it – you'd never get a word in edgeways!

Meg's family

Long Meg is a huge 'mother' stone with just that: she has 70 Daughters! This ancient stone site was built by a large community and is the sixth biggest stone circle in Britain.

The sun rises over Long Meg and her Daughters on Midsummer's Day.

How it was built

Long Meg and her Daughters is oval in shape and was built in two stages. First, a single stone – called an outlying stone – was erected. This is known today as Long Meg. Then, on a nearby piece of sloping land, a circle of 70 smaller stones, known as the Daughters, were built.

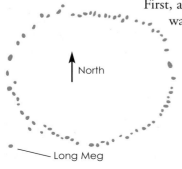

North

Long Meg

This circle is so large that over 1,500 people could have fitted inside the ring for ceremonies, even if only half of the space was used!

Like mother, not like daughter

Long Meg is made from red **sandstone**, and the Daughters are made from local **granite**. The nearest source of red sandstone is nearly two miles away from the site – quite a long way to transport a stone as big as Meg, but no doubt the builders had good reason to make Meg from this stone.

 The tallest stone – Long Meg – sits outside the main stone circle.

Meg's Daughters

The two largest Daughter stones stand almost exactly at the east and west points of the circle. They are thought to weigh almost 30 tons each! It would have taken over 100 people to move and set these two stones into position. There are also two door stones – called **portals** – that form an entrance outside the ring to the south-west. The Long Meg stone sits 18m directly beyond these portals, so we think that they were deliberately placed at this point to direct people towards Long Meg.

Leave the stones alone!

In the 18th century, a sneaky colonel called Samuel Lacy tried to destroy Long Meg and her Daughters with explosives. His dastardly plan went out the window, though, when a thunderstorm started, pelting him and those helping him with hailstones. They stopped what they were doing and ran, thinking that the storm was the sign of the devil! Local farmers have often regretted trying to interfere with stone circles. When a farmer removed some stones from a circle in Scotland, his cattle suddenly became sick. Other farmers have suffered similar fates at the Rollright Stones (*see* pages 28–31) and at the Merry Maidens (*see* pages 46–47).

Sun lovers

If you stand in the centre of the Daughter stones at sunset on Midwinter's Day – 21 December – you can watch the sun disappear directly behind Long Meg. This was probably one of the main reasons why builders chose this site for their circle, as their relationship with the sun was important. Stonehenge may also have been built for this reason as the sun sets behind the largest stones in the circle on the same day – Midwinter's Day.

The sun disappearing behind Long Meg.

This kind of rock art – also known as **megalithic** art – is very rare, especially at stone circles found in England.

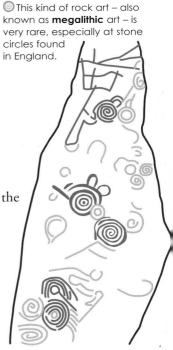

Strange patterns

On one side of Long Meg there are some markings: a **cup and ring mark**, a spiral and some incomplete concentric circles. We think that these marks have an important link with the sun. The carvings face away from the circle which could mean that Meg was erected at a different time to her Daughters. If they were erected at the same time, then the carvings would have probably faced the circle.

Two huge trees now stand in the centre of the stone circle, right next to the road that also runs through the middle of the stones!

There's no real link between witches and stone circles. The stories in this book are simply superstitious beliefs.

Witchcraft!

In the 17th century people thought that the circle was a group of mischievous witches who had been turned to stone. It was popular to blame evil events on witches at this time, and it may have been that Long Meg was named after Meg Meldon, a local woman who was accused of witchcraft. Another rumour was that Meg Meldon's daughters tried to persuade her to marry someone who was already married. As a punishment Meg and her Daughters were all turned to stone.

Tall stories

There is an old saying describing tall people as being 'as long as Meg of Westminster'. Perhaps this is where Long Meg got her name from, as she measures nearly four metres tall. One legend says that Long Meg will bleed if a piece of her is broken off, and another that the stones in this circle cannot be counted. This is also supposed to be true at many other stone circles.

Why not try counting the stones yourself at Long Meg?

Did you know?

Long Meg and her Daughters seems to be a special place that has inspired people over the years. The famous poet William Wordsworth loved it so much he wrote a poem about it.

William Wordsworth – the famous English poet who lived from 1770 to 1850.

Swinside

Age: Neolithic
Location: Cumbria
Size of circle: 28.6m x 26m
Tallest stone: 2.3m
Heaviest stone: 5 tons
Made from: granite and slate
No. of stones: 55 remain today (originally about 60)

The builders of Swinside stone circle really knew a thing or two about building jaw-dropping stone monuments. This perfect stone ring has been described as one of the most dramatic and magical in Britain.

Ⓢ Some of the stones are very close together, like people standing shoulder to shoulder.

Magical mountains

Some people think that the Swinside stones represent the low mountains that surround the site. Locals say that one of the nearby mountains, Black Coombe, is a magical place where spirits and goblins live.

Shaped stones

The tallest stone in the circle sits to the north. It's very thin, has a pointed end and stands opposite a flat-topped short stone. Both of these stones were probably chosen because of their shape and placed at the north and south of the circle for special reasons. Swinside's portal sits to the south-east of the circle and faces in the direction of the midwinter sunrise.

Ⓢ These portal stones mark the entrance to the circle.

Pebble pavement

When it was built, the circle would have been surrounded by a raised pavement of pebbles. This may have been to show people where to stand during ceremonies, or to support stones that weren't buried very deeply, like a foundation. At Arbor Low (*see* pages 22–25), the builders weren't this clever, though. Their stones have all fallen over now because the foundations they dug were too shallow.

◎ Swinside is also known as Sunkenkirk, or Sunken Church. This name may have come from a legend about the devil destroying a local church that was being built so that the stones could be used to build the stone circle instead.

◎ In the 17th century, by law, bishops had to dig up stone circles and hide the stones.

Hiding stones

The Christian church condemned people who worshipped **pagan** gods at stone circles like Swinside. Churches were built close to circles, perhaps to try to lessen the power that these sites had on people. This hasn't always been successful, though. At a stone circle in Scotland the building of the nearby church was stopped when, each night, the walls that had been put up in the daytime mysteriously sank into the ground!

Spooky stories

Christianity was responsible for lots of stories about stone circles. Some tales told of people who were turned to stone because they had done something sinful on a Sunday. Many stone circles in this book, such as The Hurlers (*see* pages 48–49), are thought to have once been people who were punished in this way – so be careful what you get up to this weekend!

Guess what?

Swinside was still being used regularly in the 1970s and 1980s by modern-day pagans and witches who performed rituals and ceremonies there – all legal of course!

Arbor Low

Age: Neolithic
Location: Derbyshire
Size of circle: 80m x 80m
Tallest stone: 3.6m
Heaviest stone: 4 tons
Made from: limestone
No. of stones: 46 remain today (originally – unknown)

*I*f you take a walk down a certain farm track in the depths of the Peak District, you'll find more than a few mucky cows in the field at the end. You'll see one of the most important prehistoric sites in Derbyshire – Arbor Low: the Stonehenge of the North.

◎ Arbor Low is a gigantic site – the stone circle is surrounded by a massive bank and ditch.

◎ The name Arbor Low probably dates from Saxon times and may originally have been Eord burh Hlaw which means the earthwork mound.

Stage 1: the cove

This large and remarkable monument was built in different stages. We think that three single **standing stones** – known as a cove – were probably erected first. Although we're not sure, it's likely that coves were used in a range of ceremonies, including funerals, and they may have been copies of entrances to earlier tombs.

Stage 2: the henge

Next, an earthwork bank and ditch – called a henge – was built around the cove. This would have been a massive job for prehistoric builders. They would have had to carve the ditch out from solid **limestone** with no modern technology or machines to help them. The henge had two entrances – a wide one on the north-west side of the circle and a narrower one on the south-east. At important times of the year, both entrances lined up with the sun and the moon.

Neolithic men clearing limestone from the ditch.

Stage 3: the circle and barrow

Then, an egg-shaped stone circle was built inside the henge. Finally, during the Bronze Age, in around 2000 BC, a round **barrow** was built on top of the south-eastern corner of the bank. This barrow was a burial mound and contained a stone-lined grave with cremated human remains inside it. We don't know who the people buried here were – perhaps they were the tomb-builders themselves, or members of their families or communities.

During the Bronze Age, burial mounds, or barrows, were built in many shapes and sizes, like these at Stonehenge.

Henges

A henge is a rough circle surrounded by a bank and ditch. The earth collected from digging the ditch is used to build the bank. Henges were mainly built instead of stone circles where there was no natural source of stone and where it was easy to dig the earth. Henges have at least one entrance and some have more than two. Their size probably relates to the number of people expected to take part in the ceremonies within their walls. The Rollright Stones (*see* pages 28–31), Avebury (*see* pages 68–73) and Stonehenge (*see* pages 74–79) are sites with stone circles inside henges. They are known as **circle-henges.**

⊚ The fallen stones of Arbor Low. Their rough surfaces are caused by erosion.

Smooth looks

The rough surface of each stone at Arbor Low was placed facing inwards to the centre of the circle. This is quite unusual because the flat sides of stones of most other circles are placed facing inwards to create a smoother look from the centre of the circle. Perhaps this means that the rough surfaces of the stones at Arbor Low had a special meaning?

Did the stones ever stand?

46 stones still remain at Arbor Low, but none are upright – they are all lying flat on the ground. Many are broken or damaged. Did the builders do this on purpose, or did someone vandalise the stones by knocking them over? One 19th-century theory is that the stones were laid flat because they were seats for Neolithic and Bronze Age people to sit on during ceremonies.

It's likely that around 250 people would have been able to fit inside the circle at any one time. That's some party!

Even though the stones are flat, this is still a wonderful site to visit.

Windy culprit

It's more likely, though, that the builders simply made a mistake when digging the foundation holes and didn't make them deep enough, so the stones fell over. The wind can be very strong in this part of the country and many of the stones have fallen as if pushed from the north, the direction of the oncoming wind.

What a find!

Excavations of Arbow Low have resulted in some truly amazing finds. These include pieces of pottery, ox bones, antlers and quite a few human skeletal remains. **Flint** arrowheads like these, right, have been found at many Neolithic and Bronze Age stone circles.

Arrowhead finds may mean that battles took place nearby or that arrows were precious enough to bury inside the circles.

Tregeseal East

Age: Neolithic
Location: Land's End, Cornwall
Size of circle: 22m x 22m
Tallest stone: 1.3m
Heaviest stone: unknown
Made from: granite
No. of stones: originally 19

Have you ever seen stones move to music? Visit Land's End in Cornwall and you might be in luck as it's home to some amazing dancing stones!

Bad behaviour

Tregeseal East stone circle – also called the Dancing Stones – was believed to be a group of naughty young girls who had been turned into stone for dancing on a Sunday. Although this belief is only a few hundred years old, it's a good bet that dancing did take place in stone circles in prehistoric times.

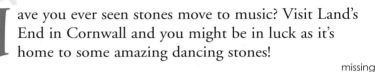

missing stone

were lying flat – now upright

North

A plan of Tregeseal East from above.

Three's a crowd

Tregeseal East was one of three circles built close together. The second circle was called Tregeseal West and the third has only been discovered recently through aerial photography. Today only the east circle survives; the second circle was destroyed in 1961 when the land was cleared and ploughed for farming. One stone from Tregeseal West still remains though and sits in a hedge nearby.

The stones of Tregeseal East are hard to find as they are often covered by bracken.

Let's dance!

Dancing is linked to many stone circles in England. The Merry Maidens (*see* pages 46–47) was once known in Cornish as Dans Maen or the Stone Dance. Stonehenge used to be called the Giants' Dance, and locals in Dartmoor call one of their circles – Stall Moor – The Dancers and Kiss-in-the-Ring. Being round, or round-like, prehistoric rings are great for dancing in. Many dances today, such as barn dancing and maypole dancing, still take place in the shape of a circle.

Wrestling in the stones

Stone circles may also have been used for other types of entertainment as well as dancing. In the Middle Ages, wrestling competitions were held each year at a standing stone on Dartmoor and were followed by a lunch-time feast of lamb. The afternoon was then spent drinking large amounts of the local cider.

Round one!

New rings

On an island in the New Hebrides, rings of stones were still being built in the 19th century. We know from historical records that these circles were used by local people to perform dances.

Tregeseal East was originally built from 19 stones – a number common to many stone circles in this region.

Rollright Stones

Age: Neolithic
Location: Oxfordshire
Size of circle: 31.4m x 31.4m
Tallest stone: 2.5m
Heaviest stone: 6 tons
Made from: oolitic limestone
No. of stones: 77

In Oxfordshire, many stone knights and their king – called the Rollright Stones – sit in a field keeping watch.

On the move

At night, when no-one is looking, these stone men move to drink from a nearby well. Sometimes they even join hands and dance. Well, that's what legend says!

In the 18th century the Rollright Stones were a popular meeting point for boys and girls, who would gather at the circle to drink beer and eat cakes.

It is thought that anyone who counts the Rollright Stones three times and ends up with the same total each time will be granted a wish.

Naming the stones

This site is called the Rollright Stones. It's made up of three different parts and each part has a different name. The circle is called the King's Men, the outlying stone is known as the King Stone and a nearby tomb is called the Whispering Knights.

Copy cat

The circle was built very like many early Cumbrian circles, such as Castlerigg (*see* pages 12–15), Long Meg and her Daughters (*see* pages 16–19) and Swinside (*see* pages 20–21). The builders laid out the stones as a perfect circle with an entrance to the south-east marked by two portal stones outside the circle. Around the circle, a small embankment was built, making this one of the few circle-henges in Britain.

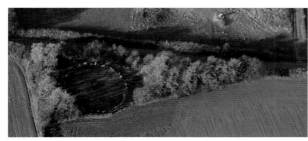

In the 1990s the Rollright Stones were up for sale for £48,000!

Ancient signpost

Just outside the circle to the north-east stands the outlying stone, which may have been the first stone erected at the site, similar to the central pillar at Boscawen-un (*see* pages 44–45) and the outlying stone at Long Meg and her Daughters (*see* pages 16–19). This stone may have been a signpost for a trackway or a settlement. It may have changed in use once the stone circle was built and, perhaps, was then used to direct people to the circle. The stone is very crooked and weird to look at and almost seems as if it could be a human shape...spooky!

Fairytales

Fairies were thought to live in caves under the King Stone, but none have ever been seen. This myth was probably started out of fear and superstition about the Bronze Age burial mounds in this area.

The King Stone. The king is rumoured to move his head for a split second during a ceremony that takes place at the Rollright Stones on Midsummer's Eve.

Look at the stones

The stones at Rollright are a type of stone called **oolitic limestone**, which is rough and wrinkly to look at. The stones sit very close together. From the inside of the circle, they would almost have looked like a non-stop wall, except for a single gap for the entrance.

Ⓢ Rollright stands at a junction of trackways that would have stretched across England. It may mean that this site was an important market place or trading centre.

Building Rollright

None of the stones at Rollright were particularly heavy. This probably means that the circle could easily have been built by a small group of people – perhaps only 20. It probably took no longer than three weeks to complete the whole circle. That's not bad, considering how large it is. So large, in fact, that around 150 people could have gathered inside the circle to take part in the ceremonies.

Vital statistics

There is a popular 17th-century story about a farmer who wanted to use the King Stone to make a bridge across a small stream on his farm. It took eight strong horses to move the stone, even though the journey to the farm was all downhill. When the stone had finally been set in place across the stream, the farmer and his workers went home, only to return the next day to find that the stone had moved! The same thing happened the next night, and the farmer thought that the stone was jinxed and decided to return it to its original place. It only took one horse to drag the stone back uphill to rejoin the circle... weird!

Legends of the stones

People once thought that the Rollright Stones were a local king and his men. According to one legend, the king and his men were stopped by a witch whilst out travelling. She gave the king a task: if he took a few steps forward and could see the village of Long Compton, she would make him King of England. The king thought this was an easy challenge as he knew the village was nearby. He took several steps forward but the village was hidden by a low ridge. He failed the task, and so the witch turned him and his men into stone!

The witch stops the king and challenges him to a task. Stragglers at the back of the group of men were also turned to stone – these are the Whispering Knights.

The witch's curse

The witch is supposed to have cursed the king with this verse:

As Long Compton you cannot see,   *For King of England you shall be none*
King of England you shall not be.   *You and your men bleak stones shall be*
Rise up, stick, and stand still, stone   *And I shall be an elder tree.*

The knights

A little further away from the main circle stand the remains of a tomb, in which a small number of people would have been buried. A section of human cheekbone was found here when the tomb was excavated. This tomb is now known as the Whispering Knights. This is because these knights are said to be traitors, whispering together to plot against the king.

There would have been an extra stone on top of the Whispering Knights originally to form the complete tomb.

Stanton Drew

Age: Neolithic & Bronze Age
Location: Somerset
Size of circle: Great Circle: 120m x 120m; north-east circle: 29.6m x 29.6m;
south-west circle: too damaged to tell
Tallest stone: nearly 3m (in the north-east circle)
Heaviest stone: more than 15 tons
Made from: oolitic limestone and **sarsen**
No. of stones: Great Circle: 27 remain today (originally 30); north-east
circle: 8; south-west circle: 11

The builders of Stanton Drew certainly took their time getting everything right with this site – it took over 1,500 years to make! The site is made up of a complex of stone circles. In fact, it's one of the biggest in Britain.

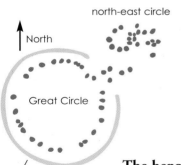

Ⓞ Most of the stones would have been found very near to the site, but the oolitic limestone would have come from over three miles away.

Ⓞ A plan of Stanton Drew.

(Plan labels: North; north-east circle; Great Circle; henge ditch; south-west circle)

The henge

The Neolithic people who started this circle first built a huge circular earth henge. This must have been a massive job, as it measures around 150m across. The bank was gigantic and the ditch inside it was 10m wide. Like most other henges, the ditch was dug on the inside of the bank. This means that it wasn't built for defensive reasons, but probably as a place for activities or ceremonies.

Timber!

Nearly 500 years before the first stones were laid, more Neolithic builders were back at Stanton Drew. This time they built nine timber circles inside the henge. Archaeologists only discovered that these ever existed very recently. The wooden posts had disappeared, but the holes they had left behind hadn't. A computer called a magnetometer was used to find any filled-in holes that were hidden under the surface of the ground. They found rings of over 400 post-holes!

The stones arrive

In about 2500 BC, Bronze Age people decided to fill in the ditch with the earth from the bank. We're not sure why they did this, but perhaps it was so the wooden structure could be better seen from the surrounding area. Next, around 2100 BC, more Bronze Age people built the stone circles that still stand today.

The stones you see today are the final phase of a monument that was constantly changing and growing.

The Great Circle

The largest ring is called the Great Circle. The Great Circle was probably built using 30 stones. Today there are only 27 stones left – amazingly only two of these are still standing. It has been estimated that over 4,000 people would have been able to gather inside it! A smaller circle was built to the north-east. The third circle lies to the south-west of the Great Circle but has been heavily damaged over the years. All 11 stones of the south-west circle lie flat.

An aerial view of the three stone circles at Stanton Drew. There is a 50p entrance charge to the circles which you can pop in an honesty box at the farm!

Avenue

As well as the circles at Stanton Drew, Bronze Age builders erected two avenues of stones. These lead off from the Great Circle and the north-east circle and then meet up close by. The avenues may have led down to the nearby river from where Bronze Age men and women collected water for drinking or for use in the ceremonies that took place in the circles. Only 13 avenue stones remain today. Perhaps over the years they have been taken away for repairing roads or buildings.

Water may have played an important part in the ceremonies that took place in Stanton Drew.

The cove at Stanton Drew.

The cove

There is also a cove at Stanton Drew made from three large stones. One of these stones is a gigantic 4m tall. Today, they sit in the garden of the local pub – the Druid's Arms – where they certainly provide something for visitors to talk about!

Wedding blues

Stanton Drew is called The Wedding by locals. A legend tells of a bride, a groom and their guests who were turned to stone because their wedding party lasted well into Sunday morning.

John the giant

Stanton Drew also has an outlying stone that may have acted as a signpost for people to find the circle more easily. Known as Hautville's Quoit, this stone is thought to have been named after Sir John Hautville.

Sir John was a huge man, and a strong and brave soldier. Local legend says that he stood on the top of a nearby hill and threw the stone (which was massively heavy) a quarter of a mile to where it stands today. In the Bronze Age, on Midsummer's Day, the sun was supposed to have risen directly behind the Quoit so that the stone was silhouetted against the sunrise.

In the Domesday Book the village of Stanton Drew was known as Stantune, which means the homestead by the stones. Drew was later added when the Drogo family moved to the area and became the landowners. Stanton Drew is now thought to mean Drogo's village with the stones.

Timber circles

Wooden circles may have been built instead of stone ones because stone wasn't available at the site. Or they may have been built first to check that a site would be useful for watching the movements of the sun, moon and stars. If the site proved suitable, then often the circle would be rebuilt in stone to make it more permanent. One important difference between stone and wooden circles was the ability to see what was happening inside. The remains of timber circles show that many are made up of lots of rings of wooden posts, each inside the other. Although we do not know for certain, it's possible that these wooden posts would have been linked by some sort of fencing or hanging cloth, meaning that timber circles would have been used for more private ceremonies than stone ones.

Grey Croft

Age: Bronze Age
Location: Cumbria
Size of circle: 27m x 27m
Tallest stone: 1.3m
Heaviest stone: 4 tons
Made from: volcanic stone
No. of stones: 12

Grey Croft stone circle has an interesting history. It was buried by a farmer in 1820, then re-built in 1949 and is now overlooked by Sellafield nuclear power station.

Grey Croft is sandwiched between the power station and a golf course.

Rescue mission

What can farmer James Fox have been thinking of when he covered up many of the stones of this ancient monument? According to stories, he decided that the stones were getting in the way of his ploughing. He obviously wasn't a history-lover! Luckily, a local school was. Pelham House School in nearby Calderbridge discovered the stones and arranged for the circle to be restored.

Buried treasure

When the stones were dug up, the school unearthed a **cairn** that contained a burial and many other items. The finds included bracken and hawthorn berries, a scraper, some charcoal, flint flakes and a piece of early Bronze Age jet. These tell us the types of things that the person buried here might have used every day, and also, because of the berries, that the burial took place in the autumn.

scraper

flint flakes

flint flake

part of a jet ring

Finds from Grey Croft, which are kept at Tullie House Museum and Art Gallery, Carlisle.

Bronze Age life

The Bronze Age began at around the same time that Grey Croft stone circle was being built, roughly 2500 BC. Farming methods began to change after this date. Bronze Age people started to use manure, which meant that their fields could be used for a far longer time than those of their Neolithic **predecessors**, because manure keeps soil fertile for longer. This meant that settlers could stay in the same areas for longer, with no need to move on to find new land to farm.

Farming was easier because of new methods and tools. As a result, fewer people were needed to concentrate on the business of making food for their families and community. Instead, they might have taken part in building communal monuments, like stone circles.

We do know things about the type of houses that Bronze Age people lived in, though. Their huts were small and round, and measured about 7m across. The walls would have been made from wattle and daub, and the roofs would have been thatched.

Although bronze had been discovered, giving this period its name, the benefits from this new metal were only felt by a privileged few because the early products made were mainly luxury items such as ceremonial daggers, trinkets and ornaments. Everyday tools and weapons, such as knives, arrowheads and axes, were still made from flint and stone.

The Bronze Age saw a huge change in the way people were buried. In the Neolithic the bones of decomposed individuals were buried in communal long barrows but in the Bronze Age round barrows were used to hold the burials of single individuals. These individuals must have been important in their community because they were often buried with precious and valuable objects.

Little Meg

Age: Bronze Age
Location: Cumbria
Size of circle: 6m x 6m
Tallest stone: 1.1m
Heaviest stone: unknown
Made from: granite
No. of stones: 11 today (originally 12)

The prehistoric builders of Little Meg decided to get arty with this stone circle! On one of the stones they made some mysterious carvings.

Naming the stones

Little Meg, also known as the Maughanby Circle, isn't far from the stone circle Long Meg and her Daughters. This is probably where Little Meg got its name from. Apart from that though, the two circles couldn't be more different. Little Meg is so small, unlike huge Long Meg, and you could move its smallest stone yourself very easily.

North

The stones at Little Meg have been moved around over the centuries.

Clumsy clogs!

Little Meg is a kerb circle. This means that the stones were once placed around a small barrow, marking a sort of border at its base. The tallest stone, just over a metre high, now lies on its side. This was probably the result of careless farmers over the years who ploughed the field and knocked over the stones – the central stone actually has plough marks scratched on its sides. How clumsy!

The circle is now a ruin, but was originally 12 stones built around a low burial mound. Inside the mound, Bronze Age people put an urn containing a cremation.

Art attack

One stone at Little Meg is unusual because of the drawings of concentric circles, a ring mark and a spiral scratched into it by the people who built or used the circle.

Another carved stone from this site has been taken to the Tullie House Museum and Art Gallery, Carlisle, to preserve it.

Other arty circles

In England, rock art has only been found at a handful of stone circles, including Long Meg and her Daughters (*see* pages 16–19) and Glassonby (*see* pages 40–41). At a circle called Goatstones in Northumberland, there are several marks shaped like a cup on the top of one of the stones.

Rock art

Patterns and artistic drawings carved onto stones – known as rock art or megalithic art – are only found at a few stone circles in Britain. The most famous sites are in Ireland, at Newgrange and Knowth, where large stones were built in circles around burial mounds. The Neolithic people who constructed these sites took great care to decorate the outer faces of the stones, although it's not known why they chose to do this or what the patterns may have meant. These decorations and carvings are another unsolved mystery about stone circles.

Glassonby

Age: Bronze Age
Location: Cumbria
Size of circle: 16m x 14m
Tallest stone: 0.9m
Heaviest stone: unknown
Made from: sandstone, grit and granite
No. of stones: 30

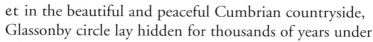

Set in the beautiful and peaceful Cumbrian countryside, Glassonby circle lay hidden for thousands of years under a large mound of earth. Luckily, in 1900, it was found and restored.

The stones today seem small and are still partly hidden by grass and bracken.

Tomb raiders?

Just outside the circle, builders buried a cremation in a collared urn. Inside the ring, in the south-east corner, they had built a tomb made from red sandstone slabs. Tombs normally contain burials, but this one was totally empty. Perhaps the tomb had already been robbed before archaeologists could investigate it fully?

Pot luck

Excavations at Glassonby uncovered this urn. You can see it, along with a bead that was also recovered, at the Tullie House Museum and Art Gallery, Carlisle.

Pots, jewellery and other trinkets really give us a sense of how people from the past lived and worked.

Mouse ears

The people in this part of England obviously liked decorating their stone circles. Like Little Meg, there is a set of concentric circles on one of the

Glassonby stones. Above the circles are two separate sets of semi circles. An archaeologist described these drawings as being like the ears of Mickey Mouse!

😊 See if you can find which stone has the carvings on it when you visit this site.

Amazing finds

As well as human burials, Neolithic and Bronze Age people often chose to bury day-to-day objects inside stone circles. Sometimes they did this underneath the stones, sometimes inside a surrounding ditch and sometimes inside the stone circle itself. Objects such as stone axes, antlers, flints and food vessels, like these from Stonehenge, have been found. Sometimes even more precious objects were buried, such as beads and buttons. These 'grave goods' may have been made as offerings to the gods to secure a good harvest or more rain to help crops grow.

Damaged stones

Glassonby has suffered much damage in the past. Over the last few hundred years, many stone circles have been damaged or destroyed by a number of different things: farming and the building of walls, roads and houses. It's impossible to estimate how many have disappeared but it is thought that it could be as many as 2,000!

Druid's Temple

Age: Bronze Age
Location: Lancashire
Size of circle: outer circle: 24m x 24m; inner circle: 8.5m x 8.5m
Tallest stone: 1.2m
Heaviest stone: unknown
Made from: limestone
No. of stones: 32

Druid's Temple site has one stone circle inside another – where this happens the circles are called concentric.

inner circle

North

outer circle

Using the circles

The inner circle has 12 stones and the outer ring has 20. Why did builders decide to build two circles like this? Perhaps the inner circle was only for the important people in a community to use? Or perhaps the circles were used at different times of the year or for separate rituals.

You can clearly see the inner and outer circles in this plan. Another stone circle like this is Shovel Down in Devon.

The blue stones

The limestone used to build the circles was found locally, scattered all over the nearby common. But the builders also used some blue stones, known as 'blue-rag', to form a layer or floor in the inner circle. These stones certainly would not have been found nearby. The builders would have had to travel

many miles to find and collect the blue rag which must have had a special meaning to them.

Quite recently vandals deliberately spilt red paint over one of the stones at Druid's Temple. Many other circles have also been the target of similar acts of vandalism.

Burial remains

Underneath the blue stone floor, Bronze Age people buried five cremations in pits. One of the burials was placed in a reddish-brown urn, although it was broken during the excavation.

The changing of the seasons must have been of great importance to the local community who built and used this stone circle because they put a tall, triangular-topped stone in line with the midwinter sunset.

Strange stones

Human burials were not the only interesting things to be found at Druid's Temple. Two unusual stones were also found. One was 15cm long and was shaped like a pear. This may have been a **pestle** for grinding **pigments**. The other stone was like an artist's palette where coloured paints may have been mixed together. A lump of red ochre was also found and this may have been one of the colours used to paint the bodies of people who took part in the circle ceremonies.

This is what the pestle and palette might have originally looked like.

Druids

It has often been thought that stone circles were built and originally used by a group of people known as druids, but this isn't true. In fact, druids were priests who lived and practised their religion during the Iron Age. This is much later than the periods during which stone circles were built. Druids also preferred to worship at natural sites, for example in woodland clearings, rather than at man-made monuments like stone circles. Authors writing in Roman times thought that the druids were barbaric, believing that they sacrificed their victims by tying them to stones and removing their guts!

Boscawen-un

Age: Bronze Age
Location: Cornwall
Size of circle: 25.2m x 22.3m
Tallest stone: 2m
Heaviest stone: 2 tons
Made from: granite and quartz
No. of stones: 19

ear Penzance, hidden snugly, deep in masses of thick gorse, lies the mysterious and unusual stone circle of Boscawen-un.

Boscawen–un from the air. The name of this stone circle means house by the elder tree.

Special stone

The Bronze Age builders of Boscawen-un placed the stones they used very neatly in the shape of an oval rather than a true circle. All the stones are local granite, except one. This unusual stone glistens brilliantly in the sunshine – it contains lots of **quartz**. Only the builders know why they chose this particular stone to be different from the others, and why they placed it where they did in the circle, as quartz stones are rare in British circles.

A Roman myth

A rather confused archaeologist in the 18th century claimed that Boscawen-un was the first stone circle to be built in Britain and that it had been constructed by a Roman! Of course, we know this isn't true – the Romans didn't arrive in Britain until AD 43.

The wonky pillar

A stone pillar stands in the centre of the ring. It doesn't stand upright, though, but leans at a 45-degree angle and looks as if it might fall at any time!

◎ Some people claim that it's possible to see two axe carvings near the base of the central pillar.

Why?

Excavations have shown that builders deliberately placed the pillar like this, but we don't know why. Perhaps it points towards a special place on

the horizon, or maybe the pillar was used in a special way during ceremonies. It may even be that this stone was the first to be placed on the site, and in fact marked an ancient track, rather like cairns of stones do today in the Lake District and other national parks.

◎ Offerings of flowers, beads and sometimes food such as eggs are made at the base of the central stone.

Meeting place

Until AD 926, Cornwall was part of the kingdom of west Wales and was ruled by the Cornish leader Hywel. The people of Hywel's kingdom used Boscawen-un as a meeting place during this time. Many prehistoric sites, including stone circles, have been used as meeting places or for assemblies or parliaments of different kinds over the past few hundred years. Some were even used as law-making courts in the Middle Ages. We don't know for definite but it is possible that stone circles were designed for these kinds of activities.

Merry Maidens

Age: Bronze Age
Location: Cornwall
Size of circle: 24m x 24m
Tallest stone: 1.4m
Heaviest stone: unknown
Made from: granite
No. of stones: 19

One of England's best-preserved stone circles is the Merry Maidens, an enchanting circle of – supposedly – 19 maids who were transformed to stone for dancing.

Dressing up

The builders of the Merry Maidens were very precise in their building of this circle. They placed the stones in a perfect circle, with each stone spaced evenly apart from its neighbours. They also dressed the stones. This means that their tops were flattened and the sides that faced the centre of the circle were smoothed by hammering them.

You can clearly see the perfect Merry Maidens stone circle in this photograph.

The Pipers

Not far from the stone circle, there are two outlying stones, known today as The Pipers. These were probably used to guide people coming from across the fields so that they knew which way to go to reach the stone circle.

This is one of the Piper stones. The Pipers are the tallest stones in Cornwall, both measuring over 4m high.

The legend

The legend that the Merry Maidens is in fact a group of young women is well known. It is said that they were crossing the fields one Sunday evening on their way to a church service in the local village of St Buryan.

Out of nowhere, two strange men appeared and started to play tunes on their pipes – the girls were spellbound, forgot at once where they were going and instead started to dance in a circle to the music. A freak flash of lightning struck and turned the girls to stone. The two musicians tried to run away, but they too were turned to stone! The speed at which the Pipers ran was used to explain why the two outlying stones were so far away from the stone circle.

Dancing is bad for your health.

Victory post

This stone circle has also been thought to be a memorial marking the victory of a battle in AD 936 of the Saxons over the Cornish. The two Pipers were thought to mark the positions of where the leaders of both forces stood when they met to discuss the terms of a peace agreement.

Athelstan, the Saxon king, and Hywel, the Cornish leader, meet to discuss peace.

Wartorn

During World War I, the farmer who owned the land on which the Merry Maidens stands decided to plough the field. Unfortunately when his workers tried to move the first stone from the circle, one of their horses dropped dead on the spot, and the farmer called off the work.

The Hurlers

Age: Bronze Age
Location: Cornwall
Size of circle: north circle: 34.8m x 34.8m; middle circle: 41.8m x 40.5m;
south circle: too damaged to tell
Tallest stone: 1.8m
Heaviest stone: unknown
Made from: granite
No. of stones: north circle: 16; middle circle: 17; south circle: 9

*I*magine being turned to stone just for playing your favourite game on the weekend! Three unique circles – called The Hurlers – on wild Bodmin Moor are supposed to be a result of just that.

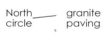 Some people believe that The Hurlers are men who were turned to stone for playing the sport of **hurling** on a Sunday.

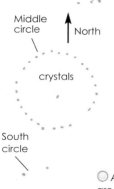

North circle —— granite paving

Middle circle

↑ North

crystals

South circle

Taking care

The people who built The Hurlers took great care over their work. They shaped each of the stones carefully before putting them in place. They also added extra decorations. The north ring is paved with granite, and there are crystals scattered in the middle circle. Perhaps the crystals are simply there from when builders chipped away at the stones to shape them, or perhaps they are there because they played a part in the ceremonies and celebrations.

All three circles are in a perfect line and are linked by a granite pathway so that anyone taking part in ceremonies would have been able to walk easily between the rings, even after the sun had set.

Stone music

Close to the central circle are two standing stones known as The Pipers. A legend says that these stones are, in fact, two musicians turned into stone for playing music on a Sunday!

The Pipers – different, of course, to those turned to stone at the Merry Maidens.

Countless stones

Legend has it that it is impossible to count the exact number of stones at The Hurlers stone circles. Despite this, one man decided to have a go. He put a loaf of bread on top of each stone and added them up as he went around the circles. It was said, however, that the Devil followed the man, taking some of the loaves away to confuse him, so he didn't get to count the stones correctly after all.

Charles II was King of England from 1649 to 1685.

Unlucky number

The Hurlers isn't the only stone circle where it is difficult to count the stones correctly. Long Meg and her Daughters (*see* pages 16–19) and the Rollright Stones (*see* pages 28–31) also share this superstition. Trying to count the number of stones at Stonehenge was supposed to bring about bad luck, but King Charles II apparently had a go without any change in his fortunes. Whether he counted them correctly or not, nobody knows!

A circle for everyone

It's possible that the three stone circles at The Hurlers each had a different function, or were used by different sections of the local community. Perhaps one circle was used for men, another for women and the third for children.

Duloe

Age: Bronze Age
Location: Cornwall
Size of circle: 12m x 12m
Tallest stone: 2.6m
Heaviest stone: 12 tons
Made from: white quartz
No. of stones: 8

The smallest stone circle in Cornwall was hidden in a field until 1801. It's called Duloe and, despite its tiny size, it's made with the largest stones of any circle in this part of England.

Heavy stuff!

Duloe is made from eight large, sparkling white quartz stones. Although the circle contains only a few stones, the heaviest is thought to weigh about 12 tons! Being this heavy, it would have needed around 50 people to shift it into position.

Duloe is the only stone circle in Britain to be made completely from quartz.

Local supplies

Although quartz stones are more attractive to look at than granite or limestone, it's likely that they were chosen for this circle because they were found close by, rather than because they are pretty. This is mostly true of other stone circles, too, where builders used local stones because it's much easier than lugging ones from further away across miles of countryside.

The different stages of a stone being moved into an upright position.

🔵 Bronze Age people were very artistic and designed many different types of pots like this one.

What a find!

In 1861, and then again in 1967, excavations were carried out at Duloe. Archaeologists discovered a ribbon-handled urn and dated it to 2000 BC. But the discoveries didn't stop there. Inside the urn were human bones, suggesting that the circle was used for burials. The urn was actually shattered during the excavation and the bones crumbled to dust when exposed to the air. Archaeological finds, like those at Duloe, are important because they tell us about the things that prehistoric people used in their everyday lives.

Treasure

A gold bracelet, known as the Duloe Torque, was found in the field close to the stone circle. Archaeologists have dated this bracelet to the late Bronze Age. It is now in the Truro County Museum in Cornwall.

🔵 This bracelet is one of the most valuable objects ever to be found associated with a stone circle.

🔵 The stones at Duloe look almost human.

Spine tingler

If you visit Duloe, you might get chills down your spine. The stones are enormous and even look like giants watching your every move... If you look closely enough you might even see the features of a face on the stone that sits furthest south in the circle!

Nine Stones, Altarnun

Age: Bronze Age
Location: Cornwall
Size of circle: 15.2m x 15.2m
Tallest stone: 1.2m
Heaviest stone: unknown
Made from: granite
No. of stones: 9

A perfect and magical circle of eight stones with a ninth stone in its centre stands in a rather lonely spot on Bodmin Moor. Funnily enough, it's called Nine Stones!

Bogged down

This circle is quite tricky to find and stands on really boggy ground. Despite being out in the sticks, when Nine Stones was built, the surrounding area was probably home to a busy prehistoric community.

☺ Cattle and sheep have rubbed up against the stones so often that the ground around their bases has been worn away and the holes have filled with water.

Lucky number 9

Many circles have the number nine in their name, including Nine Ladies and Nine Stone Close in Derbyshire, the Nine Maidens in Cornwall and the Nine Stones in Dorset. Unlike this circle on Bodmin Moor, very few were actually built with nine stones, though. When the Nine Stones in Northumberland was constructed, the builders actually used 15 or 16 stones. Today, only five remain, yet we still call the circle the Nine Stones.

☺ We know that Nine Stones was built by a large community because of the many barrows, huts and cairns found nearby.

Magnetise!

Some stones have better magnetic qualities than others. The Nine Stones at Altarnun is one of these. The stones are said to produce all sorts of strange effects on any instruments that use magnetic fields, such as certain types of watches and compasses. In fact, one archaeologist discovered that this circle has even been used to train soldiers. Army officers, realising that any compass readings taken near the stones would be inaccurate, apparently used this spot to teach their men good map-reading skills instead!

Soldiers map reading at Nine Stones.

Natural power

For many centuries, people have believed that some stone circles are magical and that they get their magic from the Earth's natural energy. Some even believe that prehistoric people would have known about this and chose to build their circles near to such places to be able to use this amazing natural energy.

The central stone is starting to lean dangerously to one side and looks as though it may soon topple over.

On the map

Stone circles were first recorded on maps produced by the Ordnance Survey. The monuments were marked as Druidical Circle or Circle of Stones, or just Stones. Not all stone circles were recorded in this way, though, and early archaeologists had to rely on local knowledge to discover the locations of many stone monuments.

Grey Wethers

Age: Bronze Age
Location: Dartmoor, Devon
Size of circle: north circle: 32.7m; south circle: 32.9m
Tallest stone: 1.4m
Heaviest stone: unknown
Made from: granite
No. of stones: 49

*L*egend has it that at sunrise the stones of the Grey Wethers turn around once, but only if nobody is there to see them do it!

Twin rings

This stone circle is made up of twin rings that stand next to each other on a patch of low ground between two hills. Their positions were obviously well thought out, because they stand almost exactly north and south of one other.

One archaeologist has suggested that the circles may have been meeting places for communities coming from north and south.

Ancient decorations

Like the Merry Maidens, the stones at Grey Wethers have been shaped and their tops flattened by the people who took them to the site. The builders

also scattered charcoal across the floors of the two circles. Perhaps they were copying communities like the ones who spread crystals at The Hurlers or blue-rag at Druid's Temple.

Perhaps fire was used in the ceremonies held at Grey Wethers. This may also explain why charcoal has been found at this site.

Repairing the circles

The stone circles at Grey Wethers were excavated in 1898 and then restored in 1909. Although the circles are not quite the same size today, they may well have been when they were built. Perhpas the 20th-century restorers were not as good at stone circle building as their ancestors!

Wether is an Old English word meaning sheep.

Sheepish tales

In the 19th century a farmer decided to move to Dartmoor and set up a sheep farm. He went to the local market to buy a flock of sheep, but unfortunately the sheep were badly bred and unlikely to make him a very successful farmer. So where did he go to drown his sorrows? The local pub, of course! After drinking rather a lot of the local cider, the farmer got talking to one of his neighbours, who said he would sell him a really good flock of sheep.

The neighbour walked the farmer to a nearby hill and pointed out a flock of about 60 sheep which the farmer could just about make out in the mist. The deal was done and the farmer paid a hefty sum of money to his neighbour. It was only the next morning when the farmer went back to the hillside that he realised what he had actually bought were the stones in the Grey Wethers stone circles – not sheep at all!

Merrivale

Age: Bronze Age
Location: Dartmoor, Devon
Size of circle: south circle: 20.6m x 17.8m; north circle: 3.6m x 3.6m
Tallest stone: 3.2m
Heaviest stone: unknown
Made from: granite
No. of stones: south circle: 11; north circle: 7

Merrivale stone circles site is impressive – there's no doubt about it. Don't expect just one circle if you visit, but circles and stone rows a-plenty!

Getting creative

The Bronze Age people who lived in the settlement close to the stone circle at Merrivale either had very good imaginations or they had travelled far enough to bring back ideas about stone circle building from other communities. They certainly went to town on this site!

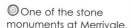
One of the stone monuments at Merrivale.

Lots going on!

You won't see just one circle here at Merrivale but two stone circles, an avenue of stones, a single stone row and a double stone row, as well as several single standing stones in the surrounding area!

A tall stone marks the beginning of the double stone row.

The cist

South of the most southerly stone row is a large **cist**. A flint scraper, flint flakes and a **whetstone** for polishing metal were found inside. There is also a huge standing stone on the site that was over 2.1m high and is now lying on the ground.

A round stone at the Merrivale site.

Stone rows

The double stone row at this site is unusual because the two parallel lines of stones are too narrow to walk between. We're not sure why builders would have placed the stone rows like this. Perhaps it was for decoration? Over one hundred stone rows are known about and the majority of these are on Dartmoor. Some are single rows of stones, others are double rows and others are built of multiple rows, all running parallel across a stretch of moor. The longest row leads up to a stone circle on Stall Moor and extends for over two miles! The beginning of a row is often marked by an especially tall stone, sometimes called a terminal stone, and they often finish close to a particular feature in the landscape, either a man-made cairn or an outcrop of natural rock.

The plague

The Bronze Age settlement at Merrivale is known locally by a different name. They call it the Plague Market. In 1625 there was an outbreak of bubonic plague in the nearby town of Tavistock and, in exchange for money, local farmers left food at the stone circle to be collected later by the victims of the plague who lived in the town. This arrangement helped to prevent the spread of the disease, which had already killed 575 local people.

Mitchell's Fold

Age: Bronze Age
Location: Shropshire
Size of circle: 21.7m x 25m
Tallest stone: 1.9m
Heaviest stone: unknown
Made from: dolerite
No. of stones: 15 remain today (originally 30)

Surrounded by tales of witchcraft and legend, Mitchell's Fold would be the perfect place to be at Halloween!

The circle

Mitchell's Fold is a large stone circle with a flat side. A single stone was placed outside the circle, and it's possible that another was also placed in the centre, but this is now missing.

It's possible that Mitchell's Fold was built by several families working together, or perhaps by the whole community.

Market place

Mitchell's Fold was built close to a Bronze Age stone axe factory. The circle was probably used by prehistoric people as a market place. Money didn't exist at this time, so people bartered their goods. This meant swapping them for other things they might need, such as axes, flint and food. Axe-hammers were very useful tools at this time and it's likely that people travelled to places like Mitchell's Fold to barter those too.

Traders barter goods at Mitchell's Fold.

It's witchcraft!

One local legend says that, during a drought and a famine, a giant lived in the circle. He had a cow and offered its milk to anyone who would come and visit. The local people were grateful for the giant's offer and made sure never to take more milk than was their fair share.

One day, a witch arrived at the circle. She decided to play a trick on the giant and milked the cow into a sieve! The poor cow tried to fill up the sieve but, of course, she couldn't. Finally, worn out, she lost all her milk, and she then disappeared – but not before the witch was turned to stone. Pictures of this legend have been carved around some of the columns in a local church at nearby Middleton. No-one knows what became of the giant...

Some say that the witch who milked the giant's cow is the tallest stone of the circle.

Did you know?

In 1907 a ball of light was seen in the sky near Mitchell's Fold, just like at Castlerigg (*see* pages 12–15).

What's in a name?

No-one really knows where the name Mitchell's Fold comes from. Some people say it was named after the giant who owned the cow. It might be that the circle was named after a local farmer who used the circle or 'fold' as a pen or an enclosure for protecting his sheep or cattle. Mitchell's Fold has also been called by other names, including Medgel's Fold and Madges Pinfold, both of which sound very similar to the name it has today.

It would have been quite a trek to get to Mitchell's Fold as it's located in the mountains over 300m above sea level.

Nine Stone Close

Age: Bronze Age
Location: Derbyshire
Size of circle: 13.7m x 13.7m
Tallest stone: 2.1m
Heaviest stone: unknown
Made from: limestone
No. of stones: 4 remaining

The stones at Nine Stone Close, also known as the Grey Ladies, are said to love to dance! Apparently they do this at midnight and at midday – but only when no-one is watching, of course.

Two of the stones are now set in concrete to stop them falling over.

Some pieces of pottery and flint have been found at the circle.

Groovy!

Some of the stones have deep grooves in their tops. Nobody seems sure why. It may have been damage caused by farming before the stones were restored or they may be a natural feature.

Great lengths

Nine Stone Close has the tallest stones in the county – they're probably as big as two of you placed head to toe! The tallest stone is bigger than it looks – over a metre of it is buried below ground.

How many stones?

Archaeologists think that there might once have been more stones at Nine Stone Close. They aren't sure if there were ever really as many as nine, though, despite the name of the circle. Indeed, excavations in 1847 only discovered seven.

Lifelike stones

There are many other stories of stones coming to life, as well as here at Nine Stone Close. The Four Stones in Powys, Wales, apparently wake up when they hear the bells of the local church and cross the meadow in which they are standing in order to drink from the nearby pool! Also, at Callanish stone circle in Scotland, it is rumoured that when the sun rises on Midsummer's Day, a cuckoo sings whilst one of the tallest stones walks up and down the stone avenue.

Nine Stone Close sits near to a **crag** known as Robin Hood's Stride.

Watch your mouth!

And talking of stones coming to life... it was thought that if you swore when you were standing close to the Druids' Circle in Wales, one of the stones would bend its head and hit you! One night, a local man who did not believe in this story decided to put it to the test and stood swearing at the stones. Apparently he was found dead the next morning...

Nine Ladies

Age: Bronze Age
Location: Derbyshire
Size of circle: 10.8m x 10.8m
Tallest stone: 0.9m
Heaviest stone: unknown
Made from: gritstone
No. of stones: 9

ine Ladies stone circle sits inside a circular bank of earth. The stones are so small you could even walk right past without noticing them!

A legend first recorded in the 19th century states that the stones at Nine Ladies were in fact a group of ladies and a fiddler turned to stone for dancing on a Sunday, and this is how the stone circle got its name.

The King or Fiddler Stone sits 40m away from the main circle.

The Fiddler Stone

Outside the circle is a tenth stone – the outlying stone. This is known today as either the King Stone or the Fiddler Stone. The inside of the circle was used for a burial – human remains have been found there.

First aid

Nine Ladies has suffered hugely from erosion and damage to the stones over recent years and finally English Heritage thought enough was enough and decided to do something about it. So now the ground levels have been raised to protect archaeology that had become exposed by soil erosion and the pathways around the monument have been restored. The result is a much prettier site and stones that are no longer in danger of toppling over!

The stones had to be roped off during the repair work to enable the grass to recover.

Protest

From 1999 to 2005 several hundred people were camped on the nearby Stanton Moor in protest against plans to re-open and expand an old sandstone quarry near the site. The quarrying works would have come as close as 200m to the stone circle and people objected that this would have disturbed the peacefulness and sacredness of the site. In 2005 the courts ruled that the quarry company could not reopen the site – a victory for the protestors!

Circle ceremonies

This site is still very important today to many different religious and pagan groups. They use Nine Ladies for many ceremonies at important times of the year, and offerings of flowers are often seen near some of the stones.

Offerings, like those at Nine Ladies, are also made at other stone circles.

Doll Tor

Age: Bronze Age
Location: Derbyshire
Size of circle: 6m x 4.5m
Tallest stone: 1.5m
Heaviest stone: unknown
Made from: limestone
No. of stones: 6

At the edge of a wood near Stanton Moor sits the small stone circle of Doll Tor. This circle is so well hidden by trees and so small, you might walk right past it without realising that it's a stone circle at all!

A small build

It's likely that only a few Bronze Age people built this circle because it is only made from a few stones. If a family or community was small then a circle could be too, as it wouldn't need to fit many people inside.

The circle sits at the edge of a wood near Stanton Moor.

Human remains

Doll Tor may have been built as a burial place. Evidence has been found that supports this theory – several urns were found inside the circle when it was excavated in the 1930s, each containing the cremated remains of a man or woman. The site also has a cairn for burials at the eastern end of the circle. In total over ten people were buried here, including a young girl.

Finding urns, like these from Stonehenge, tells us how people from the past lived.

Buried treasure

Faience beads made from glazed coloured pottery and incense cups were found with the burials and may have been left as grave goods or for use by the dead in their next life. You can see some of the finds from this site in Sheffield Museum.

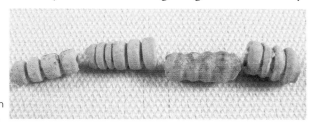

🔘 Faience beads were possibly used in prehistoric jewellery.

Fixing the stones

Over the years, like many sites, Doll Tor became damaged. English Heritage and the Peak National Park Authority restored the circle to its original prehistoric design in 1994.

🔘 Doll Tor is a pretty site surrounded by trees.

Burials

Pieces of human bone and sometimes whole burials have been found at stone circles. Perhaps the people who were buried there were the most important members of a family or a community and deserved a special burial. Or maybe they were sacrificed in order to please the gods. Whatever the reason, not everyone could have been buried in this way – there aren't enough stone circles or barrows in Britain to have buried everyone from this period of prehistory.

Some modern-day communities place dead bodies on wooden structures called mortuary platforms to decompose before burial. Hungry birds peck away at the rotting flesh, and when they are finished, the job of picking the bones clean is left to one individual member of the community who keeps his nails long for this very purpose! It's possible that prehistoric people also used this method to clean human bones before their burial in tombs or at stone circles like Doll Tor.

Three Kings

Age: Bronze Age
Location: Northumberland
Size of circle: 4m x 4m
Tallest stone: 1.4m
Heaviest stone: 2.5 tons
Made from: unknown
No. of stones: 4

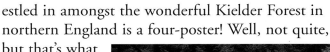

Nestled in amongst the wonderful Kielder Forest in northern England is a four-poster! Well, not quite, but that's what the Three Kings stone circle is known as. Read on to find out more!

The three kings

This stone circle actually contains four stones, although one fell down many years ago leaving three stones standing and giving it the number three in its title.

The stone that has fallen down sits at the south-east corner of the circle.

The Danish kings in battle.

Ancient grave

Three Danish kings, known locally as the Three Kings of Denmark, were supposedly killed in battle near or on this site. People once thought that the stones marked their graves. We know that a burial did take place here about 3,500 years ago. The remains were cremated and put into a small, stone-lined cairn in the centre of the circle. Whoever was buried here must have been important to have their grave marked by such enormous stones. We can be sure that it wasn't in fact the Danish kings themselves.

Four-poster

So why is this site called a four-poster? Well, the Bronze Age people who built the circle probably borrowed ideas about monument building from their Scottish neighbours. In Scotland it was very popular to make circles using four stones, which were called four-posters. For example, Deer Park, Shethin and Rouch stone circles in Aberdeenshire are Scottish sites with just four stones.

And contents that were once inside the circle's cairn – human remains or artefacts like pottery or tools – were removed many years ago.

Fake stone circles

Not all stone circles in Britain were built in the Neolithic period or the Bronze Age. In fact, some were built not that long ago. Wealthy people in the 18th and 19th centuries decided to build stone circles of their very own in their back gardens! The eccentric 18th-century owner of an island on Derwentwater in the Lake District built a stone circle next to his house. A man called William Danby who lived in Yorkshire used local unemployed men, paying them a shilling a day (about five pence today), to build an exact replica of Stonehenge, although it was

slightly smaller than the real thing. Despite the fact that they aren't prehistoric, many people still hold ceremonies in these modern stone circles. In 1861, at a national ceremony called the Eisteddfod, druids and other spiritual groups paraded around a stone circle in ceremonial dress. The 19 stones in the circle were erected especially for the festival, but the idea caught on and ever since this date a similar ceremony has taken place at the festival each year, with a new stone circle built just for the event!

Avebury

Age: Neolithic & Bronze Age
Location: Wiltshire
Size of circle: 400m
Tallest stone: 5m
Heaviest stone: 60 tons
Made from: sandstone
No. of stones: originally over 200

Avebury is one of the most impressive stone circle sites in the south-west of England. It's a huge complex made up of lots of different ceremonial monuments, including long barrows, stone avenues and stone circles.

Great Circle

North circle

North

Beckhampton Avenue

South circle

Kennet Avenue

☺ Avebury is a World Heritage Site. This means that it is protected by an organisation called UNESCO – the United Nations Educational, Scientific and Cultural Organisation.

Extending the site

The monuments at Avebury were built over a very long period of time. The builders added more features when they needed to – a bit like adding an extension to your house.

☺ Today, part of the village of Avebury actually stands inside the stones. This is the only stone circle in Britain that contains cottages, shops and the local pub!

The cove

We think that the first thing to be built on the site was a cove. It was made of three big slabs of stone and arranged in a horseshoe shape. A single standing stone was placed nearby. Next, in around 2800 BC, two circles of large, tall stones were built around both the cove and the standing stone. These are known as the North Circle and the South Circle.

This illustration shows the type of ceremonies that may have been conducted in the cove when it was first built.

Giant stones

Later on, in around 2600 BC, the builders decided to surround the two circles with an even bigger ring of stones. This circle was the largest stone circle ever built in Britain, measuring more than 400m across in some places! It is known today as the Great Circle.

Two gigantic stones mark the south entrance. They are over 5m high and are estimated to weigh around 60 tons each. This means that it would have taken more than 200 people to move them!

Most of the Avebury stones no longer stand today, but enough still remain to give you an idea of how impressive the site would have once been. And some, like these above, are massive!

Get digging

Around 2600 BC, the henge ditch and bank were built. Parts of the bank would once have stood nearly 7m high, and the ditch would have been up to 10m deep. So, the height from the bottom of the ditch to the top of the bank would have been as tall as a two-storey building! A bank this high would have prevented anyone who was standing inside the henge from seeing out.

Four gaps in the bank and ditch were made for entrances and exits.

The avenues

About two hundred years later, two avenues of standing stones were also built at Avebury. They lead away from the henge and the stone circle complex and are known as the Kennet Avenue and the Beckhampton Avenue. The stones of the Kennet Avenue can still be seen today in a field by the side of the road. They sit in pairs, so that thin pillars are placed opposite shorter, fatter stones. The two avenue stones still standing today at the end of the Beckhampton Avenue are known as Adam and Eve, or the Long Stones.

The Kennet Avenue would once have had about 100 pairs of stones in it.

The Devil's Chair.

Stone furniture

One of the stones is known as the Devil's Chair. It is shaped like a seat and if you sit in it and look upwards you can see straight up to the sky through a wide hole, rather like a chimney. Other stones at Avebury are also named after the devil – the cove is known as the Devil's Brandirons.

The Sanctuary

One special part of the Avebury complex is called The Sanctuary, which sits nearby. In around 3000 BC it was made up of six circles of timber posts and probably had a roof.

A useful place

Some experts think that the Sanctuary might have been the home of a wise man. Others think it might have been used as a mortuary. Later on, it was turned into a stone monument with two concentric circles of stone. Today there is very little to see at the site apart from markers showing where the original timber posts would have stood.

At one time the Sanctuary would have been connected to the Avebury stone circles by the Kennet Avenue.

Burying the dead

One of the earliest monuments in the Avebury complex was a burial mound built during Neolithic times, around 3600 BC. Today it is known as West Kennet Long Barrow. Underneath the long mound are five stone 'rooms'. Each one was used to bury the remains of men, women and children, and the bones of 46 people were found inside the tomb when it was excavated.

Did you know?

A female dwarf was found buried by Avebury's south entrance. It's possible that she was a sacrificial victim of the stone circle builders. The woman was buried with flints, pottery and a small ball of chalk – perhaps items that would be of use to her in her next life.

◎ Skeleton remains of the dwarf found at Avebury.

Bones!

A large number of human jawbones were found scattered in the ditch around the stone circles, but archaeologists aren't certain how or why they got there. Perhaps jawbones were considered special in some way and were thrown into the ditch as an offering to the gods to protect the monument. Or perhaps they were purposely thrown away as the more important bones were used in ceremonies elsewhere.

We know that skulls and long bones were thought to be especially important at this time as they have been found well preserved in many tombs.

◎ A skull that was discovered at Avebury. This can now be seen in the Alexander Keiller Museum, Avebury.

◎ Despite being damaged in the past, Avebury is a wonderful place to visit.

Destroying the stones

Avebury has suffered enormously over the centuries from intentional destruction of the site. In the 17th century, people were seen breaking up the stones into small pieces by heating them quickly using fire, then drenching them suddenly with cold water before smashing them into pieces. Stones in the Beckhampton Avenue were removed one by one during the 17th century so that they could be used to build local houses.

Tall tales

As with all stone circles, there have been many theories put forward about the reasons why Avebury was built. These include that it was a temple built by the Druids, a monument to a Danish king, the remains of a temple to a Roman god and a vast graveyard.

◎ Like many stone circles, Avebury was built using antler tools, like these found at Stonehenge.

The Barber Stone

In the 14th century, a travelling barber – known as the Barber Surgeon – was crushed to death by one of the stones at Avebury when it fell on him. This stone had been named after him – it is called the Barber Stone.

Stonehenge

Age: Neolithic & Bronze Age
Location: Wiltshire
Size of circle: henge: 85.4m x 85.4m; circle: 29.6m x 29.6m
Tallest stone: 7.3m
Heaviest stone: 40 tons
Made from: sarsen and bluestone
No. of stones: originally 80 bluestones and 70 sarsens

Perhaps the most famous and best-loved stone circle in Britain is the majestic site of Stonehenge. Like Avebury, Stonehenge is also a World Heritage Site.

Long-term build

Stonehenge took a very long time to make. Building started during the Neolithic in about 3000 BC and carried on into the Bronze Age. In fact, changes were still being made to the layout of the monument in 1600 BC.

Carvings of a bronze dagger and axes have been found on some of the stones at Stonehenge.

3000 BC	2900 – 2600 BC	2550 BC	2300 BC	2200 – 1900 BC	1600 BC
Henge is built.	Holes dug inside the henge to hold timber posts.	The first stones are erected, including the Heel Stone. The Avenue is built and the bluestones are positioned.	Bluestones changed for 5 pairs of sarsen stones arranged into horseshoe. Outer sarsen circle built.	Bluestones erected between the outer sarsen circle and the horseshoe.	Site complete!

This timeline shows the main stages of building at Stonehenge.

The sun shining through the stones.

Making a henge

The first people to build here, in 3000 BC, started with a henge. Unlike henges at other stone circles, the builders made the bank on the inside of the ditch rather than the outside. They gave the henge two entrances. The main one, to the north-east, pointed towards the place on the horizon where the sun rose on Midsummer's Day.

The Aubrey Holes

At around this time, round holes were dug on the inside of the bank. These are known as the Aubrey Holes, named after archaeologist John Aubrey. We don't really know what these holes would have been used for; however, we think that each hole would have held a timber post. Several cremations were also buried inside the holes, and separate burials of women and children were also placed near the two entrances.

The henge monument being built.

Yet more holes!

Next, more holes were dug inside the henge. It is likely that these were also used to hold timber posts. Like other timber circles, there is no evidence to show whether the posts that were here would have had a roof attached to them or not.

The timber structures being built.

The stones arrive

In around 2550 BC, Neolithic people began to build their monument in stone. The outlying stone, known today as the Heel Stone, would have been erected at this time. It was once one of a pair of stones that stood outside the north-east entrance to the henge. Another pair of stones was placed between these and the bank and ditch. The one remaining stone from this pair is today called the Slaughter Stone.

The Heel Stone through the outer ring of sarsen stones.

Did you know?

Stonehenge was first named in the early 12th century by the Archdeacon of Huntingdon. The shape of the stones reminded him of the stone gallows used to hang criminals and, as a result, he named the site Stanenges.

The Avenue

At around the same time, two earth banks were built parallel to each other. They led towards the stone circle from the River Avon nearby and are known today as The Avenue.

The name of the Slaughter Stone is slightly misleading – it wasn't used to sacrifice victims on.

A polished mace-head found at Stonehenge by archaeologists.

Come on the blues!

There was still no circle at Stonehenge, though. And even when 80 bluestones were set up in the middle of the site, they still didn't make a circle. Instead, they were positioned into two horseshoe shapes.

Journey to the site

Bluestones are only found in one part of Britain, in an area of south-west Wales called the Preseli Hills. The journey to transport these stones from Wales would have been a very long one. It is likely that they were moved by both people and oxen along the way.

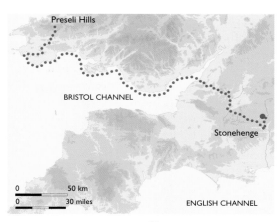

The likely route of the bluestones from Preseli to Stonehenge.

Merlin's myth

In the 14th century people thought that Stonehenge was built by Merlin the wizard and that he had made it using stones from a ramshackle temple in Ireland where years before there had been a battle between the Britons and the Saxons. The Britons were massacred, but a man called Aurelius Ambrosius, the rightful king of the British, returned from exile and helped defeat the Saxons. Aurelius decided to build a permanent memorial to his fellow countrymen who had been killed. Merlin suggested rebuilding the Irish temple in Britain – and that's where the myth comes from.

Giants!

Stonehenge was known as the Giant's Ring in the 12th century, after its mention in an important book called *History of the Kings of Britain*. Later, Stonehenge was also known as the Giants' Dance. In the Middle Ages people believed that all stone circles had been built by giants. This belief was reinforced by the discovery of fossils from early mammoths, which were thought to have been the bones of very large humans! It was also thought that the stones at Stonehenge had powers to heal illnesses and that whenever the giants felt unwell they would pour water over the stones before using the same water to create herbal medicines to cure their sickness.

New stones for old

Years after the bluestones had been brought to Stonehenge, the builders changed their minds about having them there at all. They removed them to make way for the gigantic sarsen stones that are so familiar to visitors to Stonehenge today. The builders would have had to travel over 20 miles to find these new stones, which came from the Marlborough Downs. They would then have painstakingly transported them back to Stonehenge. With each stone weighing up to 40 tons, that's some feat! Finally, the stones would have been dressed on site with stone hammers before being put into place.

It is easy to see the difference dressing made to the sarsen stones. Compare them to the Heel Stone on page 76 which is still in its natural state.

Horseshoes

Five pairs of these gigantic stones were arranged into a horseshoe shape at the centre of the henge monument, and each pair had a third stone placed across its top, called a lintel.

Stonehenge was sold at auction in 1915 for £6,600!

Lintels

Outside of the horseshoe arrangement, more sarsen stones were erected to make a circle, each pair also capped by a lintel stone. The building work would have taken a massive amount of effort by the prehistoric builders. Each of the horizontal lintel stones also had to be slightly curved in order to fit the circular shape. Even more impressive was the way that the stones were designed to fit together.

Different methods known as tongue-and-groove jointing and mortice-and-tenon jointing were used to fit stones together. These techniques make Stonehenge unique.

Finishing touches

Once the sarsens were in place, the Bronze Age people started to erect the old bluestones in an oval setting outside the sarsen circle. They didn't get very far with this before changing their minds again, though! Instead, they decided to place the bluestones in a circle between the outer sarsen circle and the inner horseshoe and this is how they are seen today. Considering that Stonehenge took nearly 1,500 years to build, it's not surprising that there were a few changes of heart along the way!

Stonehenge as it might have looked when completed.

Some of the barrows at Stonehenge.

Barrows

There are lots of burial mounds or barrows in the landscape around Stonehenge. Some are long in shape and were built in Neolithic times, but most are round and would have been built during the Bronze Age. They may contain the remains of members of the communities who built Stonehenge – perhaps the rulers who organised and led the building of the stone circle and other monuments.

The Amesbury Archer

In 2002, archaeologists discovered an amazing burial site just three miles away from Stonehenge. The grave contained the remains of a man buried in around 2300 BC, about the time that the sarsen stones were being erected. It has been estimated that he was aged between 35 and 45 years old. He must have been an important member of the local community near Stonehenge as he was buried with many precious objects, including copper knives and gold hair slides. He has been named the Amesbury Archer because several flint arrowheads were also found in his grave, as well as two sandstone wristguards which would have been used to protect his wrists when firing his bow.

One of the bluestones at Stonehenge.

The end of the circles...

S tone circles weren't built in Britain after around 1000 BC. It's possible that a change in the weather meant that some circles were abandoned as the climate got colder or wetter.

Lifestyle changes

Religious beliefs and practices may have changed, too. Perhaps some stone circles were no longer suitable for ceremonies. Perhaps people found other more suitable places to carry out their trading activities, or to celebrate or commemorate their community's special occasions, such as births, marriages and deaths. Whatever happened, these amazing stone monuments still interest thousands of people today. Stonehenge is one of the most visited sites in Britain, and attracts over 800,000 people a year.

English Heritage sites

English Heritage is responsible for looking after many stone circles across Britain, including Stanton Drew, the Hurlers, the Rollright Stones and, of course, the magnificent Stonehenge. Visit their website to find out more about visiting these ancient and amazing monuments: www.english-heritage.org.uk

Glossary

These words can be found in **bold** in the text.

archaeologist
Someone who studies archaeology.

archaeology
The study of remains – buildings, objects, human bones – that have been left behind by people from the past.

barrow
A round or long mound of earth, chalk or stone used for burials.

cairn
A man-made pile of stones.

circle-henge
Sites with both a stone circle and a henge monument.

cist
Small stone box for holding human remains, like a coffin.

crag
A rocky hill or mountian.

cup and ring mark
Shaped patterns carved into stone.

flint
A hard glassy rock which flakes easily and can be shaped to produce a sharp cutting edge. Used in prehistoric times for making tools and weapons.

foundation
Something built under a structure to support it.

granite
A hard rock made made of cooled lava.

gritstone
Sedimentary type of rock made by rivers.

hurling
An old Celtic sport played with sticks and a ball.

limestone
Calcium type of rock formed in the sea.

megalithic
Made of or to do with large stones. Stone monuments are made of megaliths.

oolitic limestone
Hard rock made of fossilised coral.

outlying stone
Standing stone that sits apart from a stone circle, sometimes marking a point on the horizon.

pagan
People who don't worship one God, but are still spiritual.

pestle
A stone or marble stick for pounding and grinding things up.

pigment
In very basic terms, this is coloured paint.

portal
Entrance to a stone circle, usually marked by a pair of stones or tall pillars.

predecessors
People who lived before us.

quartz
A hard mineral found as a crystal in some rocks.

sanctuary
A safe place, or a special place for holding religious ceremonies.

sandstone
Sedimentary type of rock.

sarsen
Hard sandstone rock.

standing stone
A large stone that stands by itself, rather than in a circle.

whetstone
Stone used for sharpening cutting tools, like knives.

Index

Picture acknowledgements

Every effort has been made to credit pictures accurately.

All illustrations © Fiona Powers 2006

Photographs:
4b, 5b, 6t, 6b, 7b, 8t, 8m, 9t, 11t, 11m, 11b, 14m, 14b, 15t, 15b, 18b, 22m, 22b, 23t, 23b, 24t, 24b, 25t, 25m, 25b, 30t, 32t, 34b, 37b, 41b, 49b, 50b, 56t, 57t, 58t, 59b, 62b, 64b, 68b, 69t, 69b, 70t, 71t, 71b, 72t, 72b, 73t, 73m, 74t, 75t, 75m, 75b, 76t, 76m, 76b, 77t, 78t, 78m, 78b, 79t, 79m, 79b, 80t, 80b © English Heritage

35b © Peter Dunn

65b © Wiltshire Heritage Museum

9m, 12, 13t, 13m, 17t, 18t, 19m, 20m, 38b, 40t, 42b, 60m, 60b, 61t, 62t, 64t © Nicola Didsbury

26b, 48t, 67t, 54t, 63t © Tom Bullock

29t, 33b, 50t, 65m © www.megalithic.co.uk

8bl, 8br, 19b, 43b © Mary Evans Picture Library

14t, 28b, 29b, 31b, 46m © Corbis UK Ltd

20b, 27b, 49t © Caroline Crewe-Read

36b, 40b © Tullie House Museum and Art Gallery

21t © Angela Lake

28t © Henry W Taunt

65t © Sheffield Museum

39t, 51b © Maggie and Keith Davison

45t, 45m, 46b © Mark Pznow

51m © Truro Museum

52t, 53m © Phil Aston www.geniusloci.co.uk

66t © Ewen Rennie

70b © Cheryl Yambrach Rose

35t © Vicky Morgan

55t © Mike Murray

12b, 44m © Last Refuge Ltd